There's Love All Day

THERE'S LOVE

Poems by California's KENNETH PATCHEN

Selected by Dee Danner Barwick

Illustrated by Tom di Grazia

ALL DAY

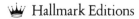 Hallmark Editions

THERE'S LOVE ALL DAY

WHAT THERE IS

In this my green world
Flowers birds are hands
They hold me
I am loved all day
All this pleases me
I am amused
I have to laugh from crying
Trees mountains are arms
I am loved all day

Children grass are tears
I cry
I am loved all day
Everything
Pompous makes me laugh
I am amused often enough
In this
My beautiful green world

O there's love all day

BE MUSIC, NIGHT

Be music, night,
That her sleep may go
Where angels have their pale tall choirs

Be a hand, sea,
That her dreams may watch
Thy guidesman touching the green flesh of the world

Be a voice, sky,
That her beauties may be counted
And the stars will tilt their quiet faces
Into the mirror of her loveliness

Be a road, earth,
That her walking may take thee
Where the towns of heaven lift their breathing spires

O be a world and a throne, God,
That her living may find its weather
And the souls of ancient bells in a child's book
Shall lead her into Thy wondrous house

CREATION

Wherever the dead are, there they are and
Nothing more. But you and I can expect
To see angels in the meadowgrass that look
Like cows —
And wherever we are is paradise
   in furnished room without bath and
   six flights up
Is all God! We read
To one another, loving the sound of s's
Slipping-up on the t's and much is good
Enough to raise hair on our heads, like
   Rilke and Owen.

Any person who loves another person,
Wherever in the world, is with us in this room —
   even though there are battlefields.

POEMS FOR MIRIAM

I

The sea is awash with roses O they blow
Upon the land

The still hills fill with their scent
O the hills flow on their sweetness
As on God's hand

O love, it is so little we know of pleasure
Pleasure that lasts as the snow

But the sea is awash with roses O they blow
Upon the land

II

As beautiful as the hands
Of a winter tree
And as holy
Base are they beside thee

As dross beside thee

[O green

O green birds
That sing the earth to wakefulness
As tides the sea
Drab are they beside thee
As tinsel beside thee

O pure
And fair as the clouds
Wandering
Over a summer field
They are crass beside thee
The hands
Move through the starhair

As tawdry beside thee

III

Little birds sit on your shoulders,
 All pure and white.
Little birds sit on your shoulders,
 All lovely bright.

Men and times of evil,
 Nothing more is right.
Little birds sit on your shoulders,
 And sing us through the night.

IV

Do I not deal with angels
When her lips I touch

So gentle, so warm and sweet—falsity
Has no sight of her
O the world is a place of veils and roses
When she is there

I am come to her wonder
Like a boy finding a star in a haymow
And there is nothing cruel or mad or evil
Anywhere

AS WE ARE SO WONDERFULLY DONE
WITH EACH OTHER

As we are so wonderfully done with each other
We can walk into our separate sleep
On floors of music where the milkwhite cloak
                                    of childhood lies

O my lady, my fairest dear, my sweetest, loveliest one
Your lips have splashed my dull house with the speech
                                    of flowers
My hands are hallowed where they touched over
                                    your soft curving.

It is good to be weary from that brilliant work
It is being God to feel your breathing under me

A waterglass on the bureau fills with morning…
Don't let anyone in to wake us.

PROMINENT COUPLE BELIEVED
PERMANENTLY STUCK TO PORCH

On impulse, to impress you, and remembering
How much in grade school you liked them,
It was I who had those thousand taffy apples
Delivered to your house—
After so many years!
Me, a humble but honest filing clerk,
And you, O little pig-tailed one, the Mayor's wife!
How was I to know you'd be off vacationing?
Anyhow, think how lucky you are…
For I might have sent roses—
And then you'd of had big sharp-nosed bees
Lappin' at you instead of them contented bears!

SHE HAD CONCEALED HIM IN A DEEP
DARK CAVE, *hewn far in the rock, to which she alone knew the*
entrance on the world, and so treacherous and uncertain was the descent
that the law-givers and the villagers passed over his head
in the clear fields above, content to allow him such safety
as he had Going to bed
And when we have done
Lying quietly together in the dark

Warm houses stand within us
Sleepy angels smile in doorways
Little jewelled horses jolt by without sound
Everyone is rich and no one has money
I can love you Thank God I can love you
All that can happen to us is not known to the guns

   Are you awake darling?
   Do not fall asleep yet
To sleep now would seem a way to die so easily
And death is something which poems must be about

But the way our bodies were wings
Flying in and out of each other...

FOR LOSING HER LOVE ALL
WOULD I PROFANE

For losing her love all would I profane
As a man who washes his heart in filth.
She wakes so whitely at my side,
Her two breasts like bowls of snow
Upon which I put my hands like players
In a child's story of heaven.

For gaining her love all would I protest
As a man who threatens God with murder.
Her lips part sleep's jewelled rain
Like little red boats on a Sunday lake.
I know nothing about men who die
Like beasts in a war-fouled ditch—
My sweet…

O God what shall become of us!

IT IS THE HOUR

A sigh is little altered
Beside the slow oak;
As the rustling fingers
Of the sun
Stir through the silvery ash
That begins to collect on the forest floor.
It is the hour
When the day seems to die
In our arms;
And we have not done
Much that was beautiful.

O MY LOVE THE PRETTY TOWNS

O my love
The pretty towns
All the blue tents of our nights together
And the lilies and the birds glad in our joy
The road through the forest
Where the surly wolf lived
And the snow at the top of the mountain
And the little
Rain falling on the roofs of the village
O my love my dear lady
The world is not very big
There is only room for our wonder
And the light leaning winds of heaven
Are not more sweet or pure
Than your mouth on my throat
O my love there are larks in our morning
And the finding flame of your hands
And the moss on the bank of the river
And the butterflies
And the whirling-mad
Butterflies!

GIVE YOU A LANTERN

Give you a lantern,
It belong to a bird.
Light on your lovely face,
O angel is such an awkward word.

Give you a sadsome tune,
Sung inside a tiring wing.
Hold it close within your hand,
Nothing'll ever seem like hurrying.

Give you a basket,
Forest keep the prettiest deer in.
Put there a bit of your heart,
Nothing'll ever harm them.

Give you a basket,
It belong to a bird.
Tell you that I love you,
O love is such a sightless word.

SHE IS THE PRETTIEST
OF CREATURES

She is the prettiest of creatures
All like a queen is she

I have made a paper wheel
And I pin it to her dress

We lie together sometimes
And it is as nice as music
When you are half asleep

And then we want to cry because
We are so clean and warm
And sometimes it is raining
And the little drops scuttle
Like the feet of angels on the roof

I have made this poem tonight
And I pin it in her hair

For she is the prettiest of creatures
O all like a strange queen is she

AS FROTHING WOUNDS OF ROSES
for Miriam

As frothing wounds of roses
Harry summer over a wintry sea,
So does thy very strangeness
Bring me ever nearer thee

As the cry of the bird-torn wind
Hastens the heart beyond its usual need,
So shalt thy dear loveliness,
Upon the forlorn unrest of my cold will,
Be as that snowy stain the roses bleed

O as flaming wounds of roses
Marry summer to the most wintry sea,
So does thy very woman's separateness
Bring me ever nearer thee

COUNTRY EXCURSION

Now this remains: the thunder stopped;
the stubborn sky grown thick,
all clumsy, holding back
and we
in silence, running, as though
on padded drums; hitting nothing,
no sound and something singing
close and hard and all around
   us, like
sudden angles loosed in wind-murdered hair.
Not laughing now, against some reason
   running, not followed
and earth
this field is dry and water needs
while drools a frivolous sky: this nasty
waiting being everything in one, a civil
war in perfect check
and then
            the rain!

It all remains: endured the shelter, and through
the limbs and leaves of chosen tree
we heard that coaxing, that definite clean.

FALL OF THE EVENING STAR

Speak softly; sun going down
Out of sight. Come near me now.

Dear dying fall of wings as birds
Complain against the gathering dark…

Exaggerate the green blood in grass;
The music of leaves scraping space;

Multiply the stillness by one sound;
By one syllable of your name…

And all that is little is soon giant,
All that is rare grows in common beauty

To rest with my mouth on your mouth
As somewhere a star falls

And the earth takes it softly, in natural love…
Exactly as we take each other…and go to sleep.

ALL IS SAFE...

Flow, water, the blue water
Little birds of foam
Singing on thee
O flow, water, blue water
Little stars falling asleep
To thy tossing
O flow, water, the blue water
What matters any sorrow
It is lost in thee

Little times, little men
What matters
They are safe in thee
O
Flow, water, blue water
All is safe in thee
Little birds
The shadows of maidens
O *safe in thy singing.*

FOG

Rain's lovely gray daughter has lost her tall lover.
He whose mouth she knew; who was good to her.

I've heard her talk of him when the river lights
Scream "Christ! it's lonely; Christ! it's cold."

Heard the slug cry of her loneliness calling him
When the ship's mast points to no star in the North.

Many men have thought they were he;
Feeling her cold arms as they held death in theirs—

The woman-face in the frame of nothingness;
As the machinery of sleep turned its first wheel;

And they slept, while angels fell in colored sound
Upon the closing waters. Child and singing cradle one.

O sorrowful lady whose lover is that harbor
In a heaven where all we of longing lie, clinging together
    as it gets dark.

23RD STREET RUNS INTO HEAVEN

You stand near the window as lights wink
On along the street. Somewhere a trolley, taking
Shop girls and clerks home, clatters through
This before-supper Sabbath. An alley cat cries
To find the garbage cans sealed; newsboys
Begin their murder-into-pennies round.

We are shut in, secure for a little, safe until
Tomorrow. You slip your dress off, roll down
Your stockings, careful against runs. Naked now,
With soft light on soft flesh, you pause
For a moment; turn and face me--
Smile in a way that only women know
Who have lain long with their lover
And are made more virginal.

Our supper is plain but we are very wonderful.

O WHEN I TAKE MY LOVE OUT WALKING

O when I take my love out walking
In the soft frosted stillness of this summer moon

Then are the mysteries all around us
O what can I say!
  the ever-known, the ever-new
  like her they seem
O lully, lullay
  only this little moment is real
Here at the edge of the world
  and the throne. The rest's a lie
  which shadows scheme.

Now gentle flowers are awash on the sleeping hill
And as I bend to kiss her opened lips
O then do the wonders and the sparklings seem
A shabby tinsel show for my dear queen.

AS SHE WAS THUS ALONE IN THE CLEAR
MOONLIGHT, *standing between rock and sky, and scarcely
seeming to touch the earth, her dark locks and loose garments scattered
by the wind, she looked like some giant spirit of the older time, preparing
to ascend into the mighty cloud which singly hung from this poor heaven*

so when she lay beside me
sleep's town went round her
and wondering children pressed against the high windows
of the room where we had been

so when she lay beside me
a voice, reminded of an old fashion:
    "What are they saying?
    of the planets and the turtles?
    of the woodsman and the bee?"
but we were too proud to answer,
                too tired to care about designs
    "of tents and books and swords and birds"

thus does the circle pull upon itself
and all the gadding angels draw us in

until I can join her in that soft town where the bells
split apples on their tongues
and bring sleep down like a fish's shadow.

O SHE IS AS LOVELY-OFTEN
And tallness stood upon the sky like a sparkling mane

O she is as lovely-often as every day; the
day following the day…the day of our
lives, the brief day.

    Within this moving room, this shadowy
oftenness of days where the little hurry
of our lives is said…O as lovely-often as
the moving wing of a bird.

    But ah, alas, sooner or later each of us
must stand before that grim Roman Court, and
be judged free of even such lies as I told
about the imperishable beauty of her hair.
But that time is not now, and even such
lies as I told about the enduring wonder
of her grace, are lies that contain within
them the only truth by which a man may
live in this world.

    O she is as lovely-often as every day;
the day following the little day…the day
of our lives, ah, alas, the brief day.

THE WONDERFUL SUN!

O *how Wonderful the Sun!*
How Wonderful the Sun!
Wonderful the Sun!
O how Wonderful the Sun!

See the Golden Sun!

The Golden Sun!
O what a Wonderful Wonderful Sun!
Behold the Glorious Sun!
O what a Wonderful Sun!

O the Sun! Sun!

See Him!
The Golden Burning Flesh of
Him!
See Him Naked There!
O the Naked Golden Wonder
Up There!
How Wonderful! Wonderful! Wonderful!

What a Wonderful Sun!

WHAT SPLENDID BIRTHDAYS

The ears of the forest
Twitch in the sun
Flies of cloud
Are shaken off so carefully

See, they alight again

In confident purity
And their wings seem to rest
Against the sky like
Candleflames painted on a cake

Deer in the sunglow

Green ears
Twitching sleepily in the warmth
Of
A peaceful summer's afternoon
Later…the herd stirs awake
Antlers purpling
And the first match

Touches the darkling candelabra

IN THE MOONLIGHT

They step through the moonlight
The cool snowy curtains
Of the moonlight
Brushing over them like wings

Of some chaste insect

And their heads
Their arching necks and flowering antlers
Are like a music
Like chimes in the moonlight

Sounding down the ghostly

Forest paths
Like trumpets made of water
Kings
Announcing a dream savior
To a world of shadows
See, they
Stride through the moonlight

Specters of the moonlight

THE BIRD-QUEEN

The swan of the heavens
Whitens the soft plumage
Of hurrying clouds
And on earth peace covers

Fields and rivers with

A meditative grace
O the swan of the heavens
Wanders upon the air
Like a queen going home

To some half-forgotten

Castle keep
O the wondrous moon-swan
Glides
Above the quiet world
Like an enchanted maiden asleep
The plumed
Headdress of her courtiers

Waving protectively about her

WE GO OUT TOGETHER INTO THE STARING TOWN

We go out together into the staring town
And buy cheese and bread
    and little jugs with flowered labels

Everywhere is a tent for us to put on our whirling show

A great deal has been said of the handless serpents
Which war has set loose in the gay milk of our heads

But because you braid your hair
    and taste like honey of heaven
We go together into town and buy wine and yellow candles

O this is celebration enough for twenty worlds!

THE GREAT BIRDS

A gentle wind blows in from the water.
Along the banks great birds are walking.
It is morning.

   Far out there are boats. It is as though
toy swans were moving their wings. It is
morning.

   Morning…oh! what a lovely morning! Slowly the great birds rise into the
soft golden air above the village. The boats
…they are coming nearer! Now we see the
tumbling glitter of fish on the decks. One of
the fishermen, seeing us, waves, calls a
greeting. Now the great birds are wheeling
and diving close in over the water. A strand of
your hair touches my cheek.

   How much better for the world had
nothing else ever happened in it.

THE FOX

Because the snow is deep
Without spot that white falling through white air

Because she limps a little—bleeds
Where they shot her

Because hunters have guns
And dogs have hangmen's legs

Because I'd like to take her in my arms
And tend her wound

Because she can't afford to die
Killing the young in her belly

I don't know what to say of a soldier's dying
Because there are no proportions in death.

WHEN WE WERE HERE TOGETHER

When we were here together in a place
we did not know, nor one another.

    A bit of grass held between the teeth for
a moment, bright hair on the wind. What
we were we did not know, nor ever the
grass or the flame of hair turning to ash
on the wind.

    But they lied about that. From the be-
ginning they lied. To the child, telling
him that there was somewhere anger
against him, and a hatred against him,
and only for the reason of his being in the
world. But never did they tell him that the
only evil and danger was in themselves;
that they alone were the poisoners and
the betrayers; that they—they *alone*—
were responsible for what was being done
in the world.

    And they told the child to starve and to
kill the child that was within him; for
only by doing this could he safely enter
their world; only by doing this could he
become a useful and adjusted member of
the community which they had prepared
for him. And this time, alas, they did not lie.

And with the death of the child was born
a thing that had neither the character
of a man nor the character of a child, but
was a horrible and monstrous parody of
the two; and it is in his world now that
the flesh of man's spirit lies twisted and
despoiled under the indifferent stars.

When we were here together in a place
we did not know, nor one another. O green
the bit of warm grass between our teeth,
O beautiful the hair of our mortal goddess
on the indifferent wind.

THE SNOW IS DEEP ON THE GROUND

The snow is deep on the ground.
Always the light falls
Softly down on the hair of my beloved.

This is a good world.
The war has failed.
God shall not forget us.
Who made the snow waits where love is.

Only a few go mad.
The sky moves in its whiteness
Like the withered hand of an old king.
God shall not forget us.
Who made the sky knows of our love.

The snow is beautiful on the ground.
And always the lights of heaven glow
Softly down on the hair of my beloved.

O SLEEPING FALLS THE MAIDEN SNOW

O sleeping falls the maiden snow
Upon the cold branches of the city
And oh! my love is warm and safe in my arms

Nearer, nearer comes the hell-breath of these times
O God! what can I do to guard her then

O sleeping falls the maiden snow
Upon the bitter place of our shelterlessness
But oh! for this moment, she whom I love
Lies safely in my arms

O MY DARLING TROUBLES HEAVEN
WITH HER LOVELINESS

O my darling troubles heaven
With her loveliness

She is made of such cloth
That the angels cry to see her

Little gods dwell where she moves
And their hands open golden boxes
For me to lie in

She is built of lilies and candy doves
And the youngest star wakens in her hair

She calls me with the music of silver bells
And at night we step into other worlds
Like birds flying through the red and yellow air
Of childhood

O she touches me with the tips of wonder
And the angels cuddle like sleepy kittens
At our side

RELIGION IS THAT I LOVE YOU

As time will turn our bodies straight
In single sleep, the hunger fed, heart broken
Like a bottle used by thieves

Beloved, as so late our mouths meet, leaning
Our faces close, eyes closed
Out there

Outside this window where branches toss
In soft wind, where birds move sudden wings
Within that lame air, love, we are dying

Let us watch that sleep come, put our fingers
Through the breath falling from us

Living, we can love though dying comes near
It is its desperate singing that we must not hear

It is that we cling together,
                    not dying near each other now

LONESOME BOY BLUES

Oh nobody's a long time
Nowhere's a big pocket
To put little
Pieces of nice things that
Have never really happened
To anyone except
Those people who were lucky enough
Not to get born

Oh lonesome's a bad place
To get crowded into
With only
Yourself riding back and forth
On
A blind white horse
Along an empty road meeting
All your
Pals face to face

Oh nobody's a long long time

PERHAPS IT IS TIME

Does anyone think it's easy
To be a creature in this world?
To ask for reasons
When all reasons serve only
To make the darkness darker,
And to break the heart?
—Not only of man,
But of all breathing things?
Perhaps, friends, it is time
To take a stand
Against all this senseless hurt.

BEAUTIFUL YOU ARE

Cathedral evening, tinkle of candles
On the frosted air
Beautiful you are
Beautiful your eyes, your lips, your hair!

Ah still they come
Evenings like chalices
Where little roofs and trees drink
Until a rude hand
Shatters them, one by one

O beautiful you are
My own
Land of holiness, unblemished grace
Springtime
In this winter place
O in the candles there
More beautiful
Than any legend's face

Your eyes, your lips, your hair!

POEMSCAPES

Selected from more than 100 pieces Kenneth Patchen calls "poemscapes,"
these short prose poems capture moods
in much the same way that landscape artists capture nature with paint.

SURROUNDED WITH ENCHANTMENTS

In the caress of shapes, colors, immaculate appearances…
O we are surrounded with enchantments!

GLAD ABOUT SEA & SKY

I am glad about this ever-changing and ever-renewing
marriage—which seems to be celebrated more out of this
world than in it. Glad of that watching blueness—which
always disconcerts the more it reassures.

A NIGHT SONG

Your letter must have pleased you to write: it's so beautifully,
so seriously petty.

SCENES OF CHILDHOOD

The air is striped like a circus tent; yellow, red, green. A great
horse with golden mane is nubbling the tops of barns and
steeples. Lovely in the tall grass…lying breathless and naked
under the hot tent… Blowing locks of bushes, king's robe-
crimson jewels flashing in the warm, silken spray…
O caressing hands of the goddess..!!

THE LATE AFTERNOON

A shadow falls across the table…drinks slowly of a cup,
nibbles the roseleaf…

GETTING UP EARLY

Such a marvelous delicacy of castles shimmering out upon
these bushes in the morninglight…

GOLDEN PLUM BUDS

Since it is as beautiful as it is, there will be nothing done in
vain in this world. When it lay across my hand, the ardent glow
of noon upon it, reverently, barely touching it, as a golden
mouth lightly touches a forehead fashioned of cobwebs,
I seemed to have entered an unsuspected portal.

THE HEART'S LANDSCAPE

In loving tenderness, whisper of flesh through the darkening
curtain… Sorrow's music taking flight through these soft
folds… In loving tenderness (and secret anguish), O intricate
intentions, banners waving above invisible fortresses…
Horizon of retreating silhouettes…

GOLDEN PLUM BUDS

And now it is your grace that I would celebrate, O my flowering one... The roses walk upon the summer breeze never more lightly than thou upon these drab lanes of the village... Village? Nay! Paradise!

GOLDEN PLUM BUDS

She loosens her hair. Out in the garden the flowers try on new colors.

LOVE IS PLAYFUL

Love is playful, noble and ennobled, O shattering gentleness! the sober, sweet glee of its flowing wonder! O love is playful and undesigning! Ah, wrath of it, the wrath of a man's love seeking its channel!

A NIGHT SONG

Your letter makes me think of two eyes, very beautiful, very thoughtful, but somehow... *only* eyes—I mean there's no face to go with them! Oh, it's not what you think—nothing *that* simple. No matter.

A NIGHT SONG

It has been a long time getting here, your letter. The leaves are
nearly gone from the trees now. Saw something today in a
shop-window which I wanted very badly to buy for you.—
No matter.

A NIGHT SONG

When did my letter reach you? Had you already found
the room you longed so hard for, or were (are) you still
looking? I told you something in the letter I didn't mean
to.—No matter.

DUST'S ONLY ENEMY

A good and gentle heart... In this world there is nothing
more beautiful.

GOLDEN PLUM BUDS

This night the wind moves almost without sound through the
leaves of the tree beneath my window. I think of many things I
would not willingly remember. The wind moves very quietly.
The leaves hardly stir.

SOMEWHERE IS FLEETING

"My" life—Out of the silence the first flakes of snow begin to fall…

A NIGHT SONG

Each step down the lane to the mailbox is a kind of hell. There in the morning…*the sun…the birds singing all around me… everything green and clean-looking*… No letter from you.— From anyone.

WONDER REMAINS WONDER

There is in each life a quality, a special fragrance of the bone and of the flesh, individual, unmistakable, exactly as it issued from the spirit's mold. A quality which nothing can in any manner alter.

THE HEART'S UNDERSTANDING

Above all I wish you joy in the things which are fashioned for joy, and an honest sorrow in what is of its nature sorrowful. Joy and sorrow—each is beautiful, and beautiful the heart's understanding of them.

INDEX

INDEX, *continued*

Printed on Hallmark Eggshell Book paper. Set in Romanee, a 20th century typeface designed by Jan van Krimpen of Holland Romanee was created to accompany the only surviving italic of the 17th century typefounder Christoffel Van Dijck. Designed by Harald Peter